COMPLETING THE RACE

Seniors in the Bible

Marsha MacLeod

WESTBOW
PRESS®
A DIVISION OF THOMAS NELSON
& ZONDERVAN

Scripture quotations are from The Holy Bible, English Standard Version® (ESV®), copyright © 2001 by Crossway, a publishing ministry of Good News Publishers. Used by permission. All rights reserved.

WestBow Press books may be ordered through booksellers or by contacting:

WestBow Press
A Division of Thomas Nelson & Zondervan
1663 Liberty Drive
Bloomington, IN 47403
www.westbowpress.com
1 (866) 928-1240

ISBN: 978-1-5127-4776-8 (sc)
ISBN: 978-1-5127-4778-2 (hc)
ISBN: 978-1-5127-4777-5 (e)

Library of Congress Control Number: 2016910575

Print information available on the last page.

WestBow Press rev. date: 10/20/2016

"Let not your hearts be troubled. Believe in God; believe also in me. In my Father's house are many rooms. If it were not so, would I have told you that I go to prepare a place for you? And if I go and prepare a place for you, I will come again and will take you to myself, that where I am you may be also."

—John 14:1–3

CONTENTS

INTRODUCTION

Some athletic races are sprints, and some are marathons. The ancient Greeks and the Romans promoted athletic competitions like the Olympic Games to prepare citizens for battle. Victorious athletes were crowned with a wreath.

The apostle Paul was quite familiar with Greek athletic competitions. He viewed life as a challenging race. Paul experienced suffering and hardships as he ran his race, yet he anticipated victory. He knew God had called him to run for His glory and would provide what he needed to cross the finish line and receive a victor's crown.

The Bible presents a number of men and women who lived long lives. Many of them lived for the glory of God through their later years. Their lives provide insights into how we also can "run with endurance the race that is set before us, looking to Jesus, the founder and perfecter of our faith ..." (Hebrews 12: 1–2).

THE BREATH OF LIFE

. . . then the LORD *God formed the man of dust from the ground and breathed into his nostrils the breath of life, and the man became a living creature.*

—Genesis 2:7

With seemingly insignificant dust, God forms man in His significant image. To create man, He chooses dust of the ground, not wood, stone, or other matter. Having already created the earth's life-sustaining atmosphere, God breathes life into man's nostrils, places him in a flourishing garden—the garden of Eden—and instructs him to care for the garden. Recognizing man's need for companionship as well as for help, God creates a woman from man.

Adam and Eve dwell in the garden amidst its trees "pleasant to the sight and good for food" (Genesis 2:9). Two unique trees grow there: the tree of life and the tree of the knowledge of good and evil. A river flows through the garden and beyond.

Descriptions of trees and gardens appear throughout the Bible. One of the psalms compares a person who is right with God to a fruit-bearing tree with leaves that do not wither:

> He is like a tree
>   planted by streams of water
> that yields its fruit in its sea-
>   son,

and its leaf does not wither.
In all that he does, he pros-
pers.

(Psalm 1:3)

In the beginning, when they are created, Adam and Eve are like fruit-bearing trees whose leaves do not wither. They know God personally, but they do not know sin, disease, or death. Aging, as we know it, is unknown in the garden.

Reflection: Have you known people whose lives continued to bear fruit in their later years?

By the sweat of your face
  you shall eat bread,
till you return to the ground,
  for out of it you were taken;
for you are dust,
  and to dust you shall
    return.

—Genesis 3:19

God tells Adam that he can eat from all the trees in the garden except the tree of the knowledge of good and evil, "for in the day that you eat of it you shall surely die" (Genesis 2:17). The word "Adam" in the Hebrew language can be an individual's name or can translate as the word "mankind."

In the garden the serpent confronts Eve and asks, "Did God actually say, 'You shall not eat of any tree in the garden'?" (Genesis 3:1). The serpent questions God's command but does not mention God's warning about the consequences for disobedience. Eve refers to the consequences, so the serpent questions God's motives.

Succumbing to temptation, Eve eats the forbidden fruit. She then offers the fruit to Adam, who eats it. Realizing they are naked, Adam and Eve hide their nakedness with fig leaves. Upon hearing God approach, they try to hide themselves from Him.

God confronts Adam, Eve, and the serpent. Adam and Eve hear

God tell the serpent that one day the offspring of the woman—the Messiah—will have ultimate victory over the serpent. God tells Adam and Eve that they have been formed from dust and will return to dust when they die. Although He exiles them from the garden, God displays mercy.

In one of his psalms, David describes God's compassion in the context of our being formed from dust:

> As a father shows compassion
>   to his children,
> so the LORD shows compas-
>   sion to those who fear
>   him.
> For he knows our frame;
> he remembers that we are
>   dust.

(Psalm 103:13–14)

Reflection: What examples of God's compassion have you observed
        in the lives of elderly family members or friends?

Then the LORD said to Cain, "Where is Abel your brother?" He said, "I do not know; am I my brother's keeper?"

—Genesis 4:9

The first specific death recorded in the Bible is a violent death—not death from natural causes or old age. Cain's murder of his brother Abel in a field dramatizes the new reality of life outside the garden. Notably, Jesus refers to "the blood of righteous Abel" when he teaches in Jerusalem shortly before His own brutal death on the cross (Matthew 23:35).

The first parents, Adam and Eve, mourn the murder of their son Abel even as they mourn their firstborn son's act of murder. The Lord banishes Cain but places a mark upon him to protect Cain from others who might attack him.

Genesis traces God's mercy and grace to Adam and Eve's family through the following years. They have another son, Seth, and Seth has a son named Enosh. The gospel of Luke traces Jesus' genealogy all the way back to Enosh, Seth, and Adam.

The phrase "and he died" first appears with Adam's death, and it is repeated numerous times as his descendants die. In the midst of a genealogical list of the births and deaths in Adam's family, the Bible presents a startling statement: "Enoch walked with God, and he was not, for God took him" (Genesis 5:24). The book of Hebrews explains why God took him: "By faith Enoch was taken up so that he should not see death, and he was not found, because God had taken him. Now before he was taken he was commended as having pleased God" (Hebrews 11:5). The distinctive phrase "God had taken him" reminds us that we can have life with God beyond life on the earth.

Reflection: What are some of your favorite songs about life with God?

A GOOD OLD AGE

As for you, you shall go to your fathers in peace; you shall be buried in a good old age.

—Genesis 15:15

At the age of seventy-five, Abram hears and obeys God's command to leave his home in Haran and go to a land where the Lord will bless him and make him a blessing. Abram journeys to Canaan with his wife Sarai and his nephew Lot, and the Lord tells Abram that He will give the land to Abram's descendants.

When famine strikes the land of Canaan, Abram and Sarai travel to Egypt, where God protects and provides for them. Eventually they return to the Promised Land. Lot chooses to dwell in the fertile Jordan Valley, so Abram makes Canaan his home. The Lord tells Abram that he will have "offspring as the dust of the earth"—more descendants than can be counted. Again He promises the land to Abram and his descendants.

War in the region leads to the abduction of Lot by enemy forces. After Abram and his servants rescue Lot and his family, the king of Salem—Melchizedek—blesses Abram, declaring that Abram's victory is from God Most High.

In a vision the Lord tells Abram, "Fear not, Abram, I am your shield; your reward shall be very great" (Genesis 15:1). When the Lord informs Abram that he will father a son and that Abram's descendants will be vast in number like the stars, Abram believes. The

Lord makes a formal covenant by causing a smoking fire pot and a flaming torch to pass between the pieces of an offering that He had told Abram to bring to Him.

Years later, the Lord establishes circumcision as the sign of His covenant with His people. He changes Abram's name to Abraham, which means "Father of a Multitude," and Sarai's name to Sarah. He promises Abraham that his wife will bear a son whom they will call Isaac and that He will make a covenant with Isaac and his descendants.

Reflection: Do you know an elderly person who has responded with faith when he or she needed to leave the familiarity of home and live in an unfamiliar place?

IS ANYTHING TOO HARD FOR THE LORD?

The LORD said to Abraham, "Why did Sarah laugh and say, 'Shall I indeed bear a child, now that I am old?' Is anything too hard for the LORD?"

—Genesis 18:13–14

Sarah was not the only one who laughed upon hearing she would give birth to a son when she was ninety years old. When the Lord previously had told Abraham he would have a son with Sarah, "Then Abraham fell on his face and laughed and said to himself, 'Shall a child be born to a man who is a hundred years old? Shall Sarah, who is ninety years old, bear a child?'" (Genesis 17:17).

Laughter often occurs when something unexpected happens. Bible scholars note that Abraham's laughter is caused by amazement, but Sarah's laughter is caused by doubt. Abraham does laugh and feel surprise, but he does not verbalize his surprise aloud to God. The Lord responds by stating that Abraham is to call his son "Isaac," which means "laughter." A generation later, God gives the name "Israel" to Jacob, the grandson of Abraham and Sarah.

After Isaac's birth, Sarah acknowledges godly laughter: "God has made laughter for me; everyone who hears will laugh over me" (Genesis 21:6). Although her initial laugh conveyed doubt, now she laughs with amazement and laughs with others. In the years that follow Isaac's birth, when Abraham and Sarah speak Isaac's name, undoubtedly they often recall God's reason for giving their son his name.

Reflection: Have you heard of a surprising circumstance in the life of a senior that has caused you or others to laugh with amazement?

YOUR ONLY SON ISAAC WHOM YOU LOVE

Day 6

He said, "Take your son, your only son Isaac, whom you love, and go to the land of Moriah, and offer him there as a burnt offering on one of the mountains of which I shall tell you."

—Genesis 22:2

Years earlier, Sarah had urged Abraham to father a child with Hagar, her handmaiden, but conflict developed between the two women after Hagar gave birth to Ishmael. Sarah finally demanded that Abraham send away Hagar and Ishmael, and God told Abraham to listen to Sarah, his wife. Abraham trusted God and sent away his son Ishmael with Ishmael's mother, Hagar, into the wilderness.

Now, years later, Abraham hears God command him to do the unthinkable—to offer his son Isaac as a burnt offering. Nevertheless, Abraham obeys: "He considered that God was able even to raise him [Isaac] from the dead, from which, figuratively speaking, he did receive him back" (Hebrews 11:19).

As father and son approach the place where Abraham will build an altar for the sacrifice, Isaac asks what lamb will be offered since they are not bringing an animal to sacrifice. Abraham replies, "God will provide for himself the lamb for a burnt offering, my son" (Genesis 22:8).

Abraham binds Isaac on the altar and prepares to slay his son with his knife. However, God stops the sacrifice and provides a ram for the burnt offering. Abraham offers the ram and names the place "The LORD will provide." Long afterwards, in His appointed time, God provides His own Son as the Lamb of God for us—a sacrificial offering for our sin.

This ultimate test of Abraham's faith in God's provision comes late in his life. Subsequently the Lord tells him, "[A]nd in your offspring shall all the nations of the earth be blessed, because you have obeyed my voice" (Genesis 22:18).

Reflection: When have you seen God provide for an elderly person unable to provide for himself or herself?

TO MOURN FOR SARAH

And Sarah died at Kiriath-arba (that is, Hebron) in the land of Canaan, and Abraham went in to mourn for Sarah and to weep for her.

—Genesis 23:2

Sarah lives thirty-six years after giving birth to Isaac and enjoys a relationship with her son. When she dies, Abraham mourns and negotiates to buy a cave and the field around it as a family burial site. Even though the Canaanites who own the site offer to give him the cave and field, Abraham insists on buying the property formally with a significant amount of silver. A deed is prepared, and Abraham purchases the field, the cave, and the trees in the field. Then Abraham buries the body of Sarah in the cave.

Earlier in their lives, when famine in Canaan caused Abraham and Sarah to journey to Egypt, Abraham asked Sarah to say she was his sister so the Egyptians would not kill him in order to possess her. Pharaoh was interested in Abraham's beautiful wife; however, God intervened, and Abraham and Sarah returned to Canaan. Years later, sojourning in Gerar, Abraham again asked Sarah to pose as his sister. Once again God intervened, rescued Sarah, and preserved their marriage relationship. In death, the bodies of Abraham and Sarah lie together in a family burial site in the land God promised to their descendants.

The book of Hebrews lists Abraham as a man of faith and also

Sarah as a woman of faith: "By faith Sarah herself received power to conceive, even when she was past the age, since she considered him faithful who had promised" (Hebrews 11:11).

The Bible offers a poignant insight into Isaac's emotions at his mother's death: "Then Isaac brought her [Rebekah] into the tent of Sarah his mother and took Rebekah, and she became his wife, and he loved her. So Isaac was comforted after his mother's death" (Genesis 24:67).

Reflection: Do you have an idea for a place to bury a body or scatter ashes?

WHILE HE WAS STILL LIVING

Abraham gave all he had to Isaac. But to the sons of his concubines Abraham gave gifts, and while he was still living he sent them away from his son Isaac, eastward to the east country.

—Genesis 25:5–6

After Sarah dies, Abraham has several sons with Keturah. The Bible records that he "gave all he had to Isaac," and "to the sons of his concubines Abraham gave gifts." Wisely Abraham relocates the concubines' sons in the east at a distance from Isaac's land. Abraham is seeking to prevent conflict and to provide for the well-being of everyone in his family after his death. As God promised, Abraham dies "in a good old age, an old man and full of years, and was gathered to his people" (Genesis 25:8).

Abraham's son Ishmael, by Sarah's maid Hagar, returns for Abraham's burial. Decades have passed since God told Abraham to send Ishmael and Hagar away into the wilderness. God has provided for Ishmael through the years: "And God was with the boy, and he grew up. He lived in the wilderness and became an expert with the bow" (Genesis 21:20).

Now the two sons, Isaac and Ishmael, together bury their father in the cave purchased by Abraham as the family burial site. The Bible simply mentions Ishmael's presence at the burial: "Isaac and Ishmael his sons buried him in the cave of Machpelah" (Genesis 25:9).

The genealogies for Ishmael and Isaac are given in the Bible.

Ishmael has twelve sons, and Isaac has two—Jacob and Esau. Jacob, called Israel, has twelve sons. Esau has five.

Reflection: Have you observed parents bless the members of their family by leaving words of love or a gift of love to each one?

THAT MY SOUL MAY BLESS YOU

He [Isaac] said, "Behold, I am old; I do not know the day of my death. Now then, take your weapons, your quiver and your bow, and go out to the field and hunt game for me, and prepare for me delicious food, such as I love, and bring it to me so that I may eat, that my soul may bless you before I die."

—Genesis 27:2–4

Thinking his death might be approaching, Isaac tells his son Esau that the time seems right to give the anticipated blessing for the firstborn son. However, Rebekah instructs their son Jacob to pretend to be Esau so Jacob can receive that blessing. Jacob succeeds in deceiving his elderly, blind father.

Rebekah hears that Esau is furious about his brother's deception and intends to kill Jacob when their father dies. She urges Jacob to flee to the home of her brother, Laban, in distant Haran. Rebekah then declares to her husband that she despairs of Jacob finding a wife who is not a Hittite. So Isaac sends Jacob to seek a wife amidst family in Haran. Rebekah hopes that Esau's anger will subside and Jacob will be able to return home. As Jacob travels to his uncle's home, the Lord encourages him in a dream that he will inherit the land on which he is lying and will have many descendants. The Bible does not record that Rebekah ever saw Jacob again.

Isaac lives for many years with the memory that his younger son, Jacob, deceived him and stole the blessing intended for the firstborn son. Upon Jacob's return to Canaan years later, Jacob reconciles with Esau and visits his father's house again. When Isaac dies, Jacob and Esau together bury their father: "And Isaac breathed his last, and he died and was gathered to his people, old and full of days. And his sons Esau and Jacob buried him" (Genesis 35:29).

Jesus, responding to a question about the resurrection of the dead, presents Abraham, Isaac, and Jacob as an example of resurrection: "But that the dead are raised, even Moses showed, in the passage about the bush, where he calls the Lord the God of Abraham and the God of Isaac and the God of Jacob. Now he is not God of the dead, but of the living, for all live to him" (Luke 20:37–38).

Reflection: Do you know a senior who has seen healing between family members late in life?

I WILL GO

Day 10

But when they told him all the words of Joseph, which he had said to them, and when he saw the wagons that Joseph had sent to carry him, the spirit of their father Jacob revived. And Israel said, "It is enough; Joseph my son is still alive. I will go and see him before I die."

—Genesis 45:27–28

Jacob, given the name "Israel" by God, encounters deception in the years following his deception of his father, Isaac. Jacob's father-in-law, Laban, deceives Jacob by sending Leah, the older daughter, instead of Rachel, into Jacob's tent on his wedding night. As the years pass, Jacob has twelve sons. The sons of Jacob deceive their father into thinking that his beloved son Joseph has been killed by a wild beast. Rejecting his family's attempts to comfort him, Jacob declares, "No, I shall go down to Sheol to my son, mourning" (Genesis 37:35).

Many years later, upon realizing that Joseph is alive in Egypt, Jacob makes the arduous journey to Egypt, traveling in a wagon. All that matters to him is the opportunity to see the son whom he has been mourning for years. God encourages Jacob in a nighttime vision, telling him He will be with Jacob in Egypt and letting him know Joseph will close Jacob's eyes when he dies.

In Egypt, Jacob discovers two grandsons he did not know he had—Joseph's sons, Ephraim and Manasseh. Jacob lives the next seventeen years with his family in the land of Goshen in Egypt.

As death approaches, Jacob speaks prophetically to each of his sons. His final words to Judah include a prophetic reference to the Messiah:

> The scepter shall not depart
>   from Judah,
>   nor the ruler's staff from
>   between his feet,
> until tribute comes to him;
>   and to him shall be the obe-
>   dience of the peoples.

(Genesis 49:10)

He instructs his sons to bury him in the cave where Abraham, Sarah, Isaac, Rebekah, and Leah are buried.

Upon his father's death, Joseph orders the body embalmed. With Pharaoh's permission, Joseph and his brothers travel in an elaborate funeral procession to Canaan to bury their father as he requested. Then Joseph and his brothers return to Egypt.

Reflection: What would you do if you learned that a son or daughter had not died but was alive in a distant country?

GOD WILL VISIT YOU   *Day 11*

> *And Joseph said to his brothers, "I am about to die, but God will visit you and bring you up out of this land to the land that he swore to Abraham, to Isaac, and to Jacob."*

—Genesis 50:24

In his early years, Joseph is betrayed by his brothers, sold into slavery, and wrongly imprisoned by his Egyptian master. God gives Pharaoh two disturbing dreams and enables Joseph to interpret them. Joseph tells Pharaoh the dreams warn that seven years of famine will come after seven years of plenty. Pharaoh then places Joseph in a position of power, second only to Pharaoh, to prepare Egypt for the years ahead. After famine grips the land of Canaan, Joseph's brothers travel to Egypt to buy food. They unknowingly encounter Joseph, and God reunites Joseph with his family through a series of events displaying God's faithfulness.

When Joseph and his brothers bury their father, Jacob, in Canaan, Joseph tells his brothers, "As for you, you meant evil against me, but God meant it for good, to bring it about that many people should be kept alive, as they are today" (Genesis 50:20). Joseph reassures them that he will continue to take care of them and their children. In his later years, Joseph is surrounded by family, including beloved grandchildren.

As he is dying, Joseph prophesies that God will bring the people of Israel back to the land He promised to Abraham, Isaac, and Jacob.

Joseph commands the sons of Israel to take an oath that they will carry his bones with them when they return to the Promised Land.

Four hundred years later, the Lord leads Moses and the children of Israel out of Egypt and through the wilderness. They carry the bones of Joseph with them for forty years. Arriving in the Promised Land, they bury Joseph's bones as Joseph had made the sons of Israel swear to do.

Reflection: If you have attended a graveside memorial service, what did you most appreciate?

EIGHTY YEARS OLD

Now Moses was eighty years old, and Aaron eighty-three years old, when they spoke to Pharaoh.

—Exodus 7:7

Rescued as a baby and adopted by Pharaoh's daughter, Moses lives for about forty years in Pharaoh's household. After Moses is observed killing an Egyptian who is beating a Hebrew slave, Moses knows Pharaoh will seek to kill him. He flees to Midian, marries a Midianite, and shepherds his father-in-law's sheep for many years. Shepherding sheep becomes preparation for shepherding the people of Israel.

When Moses is eighty years old, God calls out to Moses from a burning bush and declares that Moses is going to lead the people of Israel out of their bondage in Egypt. The Lord shows him miraculous signs, but Moses feels inadequate and responds that he is "slow of speech and of tongue" (Exodus 4:10).

The Lord replies that Moses can tell His words to his brother, Aaron, who then can speak His words to the people of Israel. A momentous struggle is about to begin, but the Lord assures Moses that He will teach Moses and Aaron what needs to be done.

In Psalm 90, Moses contrasts God's everlasting existence to the short lifespan of a man. Moses refers to the later years of life—seventy years and eighty years—as times of "toil and trouble." He concludes his psalm by asking for the Lord's help:

28

Let your work be shown to
　　your servants,
　and your glorious power to
　　their children.
Let the favor of the Lord our
　　God be upon us,
　and establish the work of
　　our hands upon us;
　yes, establish the work of
　　our hands!

(Psalm 90:16–17)

Reflection: What work of your hands for the Lord would you like
　　Him to establish for you as you grow older?

THE LORD WILL FIGHT FOR YOU   *Day 13*

> *And Moses said to the people, "Fear not, stand firm, and see the*
> *salvation of the LORD, which He will work for you today. For*
> *the Egyptians whom you see today, you shall never see again. The*
> *LORD will fight for you, and you have only to be silent."*

—Exodus 14:13–14

Even the strongest among the people of Israel realize they are no match for Pharaoh's military with its chariots. The Israelites have survived suffering and degradation for generations. Now they fear they will die violent deaths alongside their families. Although they recently witnessed the Lord's power as He brought ten plagues against Egypt, they complain sarcastically to Moses as they see Pharaoh's army approaching: "Is it because there are no graves in Egypt that you have taken us away to die in the wilderness?" (Exodus 14:11).

The elderly have endured in survival mode for years, cowering before their slave masters and depending upon themselves. Moses answers the bitter words of former slaves by asserting that the Lord will fight for them and they will see His salvation.

The Lord divides the Red Sea and turns its sea floor into dry land. Terrified of the Egyptians and their chariots, the people of Israel choose to walk at night between towering walls of water formed by God. They fear the Egyptians more than the walls of water.

In the morning the people fear the Lord when they watch the walls of water engulf Pharaoh's horses, chariots, and horsemen. The elderly

Israelites see Almighty God vanquish their lifelong enemy and deliver the people of Israel in a way they never could have imagined. Young and old together witness God's deliverance.

Reflection: Has there been a time in your life when you could not protect yourself from danger, but the Lord delivered you?

THE LORD IS MY STRENGTH AND MY SONG

I will sing to the LORD, for

he has triumphed glori-

ously;

the horse and his rider he

has thrown into the sea.

The LORD is my strength and

my song,

and he has become my sal-

vation;

this is my God, and I will

praise him;

my father's God, and I will

exalt him.

—Exodus 15:1–2

Singing on the shores of the Red Sea, the people of Israel praise God that He has delivered them from "the horse and his rider." Moses' sister, Miriam, leads the women as they pick up tambourines and dance.

About eighty years earlier, Miriam had watched over her baby brother when he was three months old. Their mother had hidden him in a basket among reeds in the river. God protected the baby boy from

Pharaoh's soldiers, who had orders to kill the newborn sons of the people of Israel. Pharaoh's daughter found the baby and later adopted him as her son. Since she had drawn him out of the water, she named him Moses, which can translate as "he who draws out." Now Miriam in her eighties sees God use her brother to draw the Israelites out of the Red Sea and deliver them from Pharaoh's soldiers.

In their song of deliverance, the people anticipate the Lord leading them back to the land of their forefathers and "planting" them there. They affirm their connection with those who have suffered and lived before them. Standing on the shore of the Red Sea, they proclaim that the God of their forefathers is also their strength, song, and salvation. Now after four hundred years they taste freedom.

Reflection: What are some of your favorite songs about Almighty God's power?

HONOR THE FACE OF AN OLD MAN

You shall stand up before the gray head and honor the face of an old man, and you shall fear your God: I am the LORD.

—Leviticus 19:32

Rising in the presence of the gray head acknowledges the years of experience and wisdom that God has given. As the people of Israel journey toward the Promised Land, unfortunately they disrespect the elderly Moses and disrespect God. Consequences follow.

After their victory at the Red Sea, the Israelites follow Moses into the wilderness for three days but do not find water for themselves and their livestock. Arriving at Marah, they do find water, but it is bitter. Bitterly they complain to Moses, and the Lord directs Moses to throw a specific tree into the water. The water then becomes sweet.

The people become hungry, and their faith is tested again. Their complaints assert that they would have preferred to die as slaves eating well in Egypt rather than free people starving in the wilderness. They focus on their former food—pots of meat and an abundance of bread.

The Lord tells Moses that He is "about to rain bread from heaven" (Exodus 16:4). He sends quail, and the Lord provides manna for the people to gather each morning. On the sixth day He provides enough manna for that day and the Sabbath. At first, some of them ignore God's instructions for gathering the manna. Much later, some even complain about God's provision of manna: "[T]here is nothing at all but this manna to look at" (Numbers 11:6).

Faithfully God provides daily manna throughout their forty-year journey. After they cross into the Promised Land and keep the Passover on the plains of Jericho, the following day they eat the produce of the land. The manna never reappears.

Time after time, the people of Israel fail to trust Moses and the Lord, even asking, "Is the LORD among us or not?" (Exodus 17:7). Time after time, Moses faithfully intercedes for them before the Lord.

Reflection: What might have been some of the challenges that the elderly, in particular, experienced on their forty-year journey?

GRAY HAIR *Day 16*

Gray hair is a crown of glory;
it is gained in a righteous life.

—Proverbs 16:31

When God makes Himself known to Moses at the burning bush, He calls him to lead Israel out of bondage. Moses returns to Egypt with his family, but later he sends his wife and sons back to Jethro, his father-in-law in Midian. Upon hearing that God delivered Moses and the Israelites out of Egypt and enabled them to defeat Amalek, Jethro brings Moses' family to him in the wilderness. Moses shows the utmost respect for his elderly father-in-law.

In the camp, Jethro notices that Moses is trying to judge all disputes arising among the people of Israel. Moses' father-in-law offers a practical alternative. He advises Moses to choose men of integrity to judge less important matters, leaving Moses free to judge the more complex disputes. The Bible records that Moses implements his father-in-law's advice. Moses, an elderly man who listens to God, also listens to the godly advice of his elderly father-in-law. Everyone benefits.

On their journey to the Promised Land, the Israelites camp before Mount Sinai. The Lord presents to them the Ten Commandments with its commandment to honor their fathers and mothers "that your days may be long in the land that the LORD your God is giving you"

(Exodus 20:12). The people understand that honoring the elderly honors the Lord.

A number of proverbs in the Bible present old age as one of life's blessings when a person has walked in the path of wisdom. Gray or silver-colored hair is viewed as similar to "a crown of glory" (Proverbs 16:31), and grandchildren as "the crown of the aged" (Proverbs 17:6).

Reflection: Describe wise advice you have received from a senior— advice that benefitted you immensely.

THEY WOULD SET OUT

Whether it was two days, or a month, or a longer time that the cloud continued over the tabernacle, abiding there, the people of Israel remained in camp and did not set out, but when it lifted they would set out.

—Numbers 9:22

The people of Israel never know ahead of time how long they will camp in any location. The elderly, who once knew familiar routines as slaves in Egypt, find themselves learning very different routines late in life. They gaze at the cloud above the tabernacle. Along with their family and friends, they wait and wonder when they will be continuing their journey as well as what they will encounter next.

They have exchanged Pharaoh for Moses, slave quarters for tents, a variety of foods for manna, water from the Nile River for water from a rock or other sources, and the expectation of a grave in Egypt for a grave in a foreign land. They struggle with trusting and obeying God. Though no longer accountable to human masters, they are accountable to their Creator.

Psalm 78, written by Asaph, recounts the mercy the Lord showed to the people of Israel on their journey to the Promised Land:

> Yet he, being compassionate,
>   atoned for their iniquity
>   and did not destroy them;

he restrained his anger often
and did not stir up all his
wrath.
He remembered that they
were but flesh,
a wind that passes and
comes not again.

(Psalm 78:38–39)

Although they were unfaithful at times to God, God remained faithful to them.

Reflection: Do you know a senior who learned late in life to trust God in extremely challenging circumstances?

AARON RAN

And Moses said to Aaron, "Take your censer, and put fire on it from off the altar and lay incense on it and carry it quickly to the congregation and make atonement for them, for wrath has gone out from the LORD; the plague has begun." So Aaron took it as Moses said and ran into the midst of the assembly. And behold, the plague had already begun among the people. And he put on the incense and made atonement for the people. And he stood between the dead and the living, and the plague was stopped.

—Numbers 16:46–48

During the years when Moses is living in Pharaoh's household and later in Midian, Aaron marries and has four sons in Egypt. When Moses, Aaron, and their sister, Miriam, are in their eighties, the Lord reunites them. God appoints Aaron as the high priest.

The book of Numbers relates the intercession of Moses and Aaron after Korah and others reject the leadership of Moses and Aaron. Even though the Lord causes an earthquake to swallow Korah and other rebellious leaders, along with their households, the next day the people of Israel continue to criticize Moses and Aaron. When the Lord tells Moses to stand aside so that He "may consume them in a moment," Moses and Aaron "fell on their faces" (Numbers 16:45).

Moses urges Aaron, who is in his eighties, to hurry into the assembly with a censer containing fire from the altar and incense to halt the terrible plague resulting from the people's disobedience. The elderly Aaron runs. Placing fire and incense in his censer, he stands "between the dead and the living," and the plague is halted. The elderly high priest has interceded for rebellious people who could not intercede for themselves.

Reflection: Have you been encouraged to know an older person who intercedes in prayer for others or for you?

MOSES AND AARON GATHERED THE ASSEMBLY

Day 19

Then Moses and Aaron gathered the assembly together before the rock, and he [Moses] said to them, "Hear now, you rebels: shall we bring water for you out of this rock?" And Moses lifted up his hand and struck the rock with his staff twice, and water came out abundantly, and the congregation drank, and their livestock. And the LORD said to Moses and Aaron, "Because you did not believe in me, to uphold me as holy in the eyes of the people of Israel, therefore you shall not bring this assembly into the land that I have given them."

—Numbers 20:10–12

Moses knew better. After walking with God and experiencing His faithfulness, Moses speaks and acts at Meribah contrary to all he has learned. The Lord instructs him to provide water for His people simply by speaking to the rock. Instead, Moses says, "Hear now, you rebels: shall we bring water for you out of this rock?" He then strikes the rock twice.

Exasperated and angry, Moses has good reason to feel frustrated with the people the Lord has called him to lead. However, he dishonors the Lord before His people, and the Lord holds Moses accountable.

At Kadesh, the people had not heeded Joshua and Caleb when they returned from exploring the Promised Land with ten other spies. Joshua and Caleb urged the people to trust God and enter the land, but the other ten insisted that entering the land would bring disaster upon all of them. The people refused to enter, so the Lord declared that none of their generation would enter the Promised Land except for Joshua and Caleb. That generation would wander in the wilderness for forty years—one year for each of the days that the spies had explored the land.

Now Moses and Aaron will not enter. However, although Moses and Aaron dishonor the Lord in public at Meribah, the Lord blesses His two servants in their final days of life as the people of Israel approach the Promised Land.

Reflection: Can you recall an incident in which an older person was patient with you when he or she had good reason to feel exasperation?

ON ELEAZAR HIS SON

Moses did as the LORD commanded. And they went up Mount Hor in the sight of all the congregation. And Moses stripped Aaron of his garments and put them on Eleazar his son. And Aaron died there on the top of the mountain. Then Moses and Eleazar came down from the mountain. And when all the congregation saw that Aaron had perished, all the house of Israel wept for Aaron thirty days.

—Numbers 20:27–29

Aaron prepares for his death as he climbs Mount Hor with his son and brother. Moses removes Aaron's priestly garments, which are to be worn only by a high priest, and places the garments upon Eleazar, Aaron's son.

Earlier in Aaron's life, two of his sons, Nadab and Abihu, died when they foolishly presented fire and incense in their censers to the Lord in a manner He had not prescribed. Now at the end of his life, Aaron is blessed to see one of his sons standing before him clothed in the garments Aaron has worn as the high priest.

Like Moses, Aaron will not enter the Promised Land because he did not honor the Lord at Meribah when the Lord told Moses to provide water by speaking to a rock. Aaron's years of serving the Lord as high priest end quietly on a mountaintop with his brother and a son. His sister, Miriam, had died earlier in Kadesh.

In the book of Micah, the Lord acknowledges all three siblings—Moses, Aaron, and Miriam—for their role in bringing the people of Israel out of bondage:

> For I brought you up from
>   the land of Egypt,
>   and redeemed you from the
>   house of slavery,
>   and I sent before you Moses,
>   Aaron, and Miriam.

(Micah 6:4)

Reflection: Do you know elderly men and women who have been blessed to see their adult children serving the Lord in ministry?

THE LAND THAT YOU SHALL SEE *Day 21*

Go up to the top of Pisgah and lift up your eyes westward and northward and southward and eastward, and look at it with your eyes, for you shall not go over this Jordan. But charge Joshua, and encourage and strengthen him, for he shall go over at the head of this people, and he shall put them in possession of the land that you shall see.

—Deuteronomy 3:27–28

In a nation or in a family, the time comes when authority must transfer to another person. After forty years of leading the people of Israel, Moses pleads with the Lord to allow him to see the richness of the Promised Land. Due to Moses' disobedience at Meribah, the Lord tells him he will not be allowed to enter the land, but he will be allowed to see it. Joshua will lead the people across the Jordan and into the Promised Land. The Lord instructs Moses to encourage and strengthen Joshua for his new role.

Moses publicly transfers authority to Joshua, telling him in front of the people of Israel to be "strong and courageous" (Deuteronomy 31:7). Moses emphasizes that the Lord will cross into the land with them and will not leave them. Thus they should not be afraid or allow themselves to become discouraged by the struggles they will face.

Aware that the Israelites will encounter numerous challenges and succumb to temptations, Moses shares a final song and a blessing.

The song includes words of warning, but also a reminder of God's faithfulness to His people:

> But the LORD's portion is his
>   people,
>   Jacob his allotted heritage.
> He found him in a desert
>   land,
>   and in the howling waste of
>   the wilderness;
> he encircled him, he cared for
>   him,
>   he kept him as the apple of
>   his eye.

(Deuteronomy 32:9–10)

Reflection: If you had the opportunity to share with family and friends some final words about God's faithfulness to you, what would you say?

*So Moses the servant of the LORD died there in the land of Moab,
according to the word of the LORD, and he buried him in the
valley in the land of Moab opposite Beth-peor; but no one knows
the place of his burial to this day. Moses was 120 years old when
he died. His eye was undimmed, and his vigor unabated.*

—Deuteronomy 34:5–7

After Moses' final words to the people whom he has led for so
many years, he climbs to the top of Pisgah by himself. He still has
good eyesight, and so he is able to see the panoramic view of the
Promised Land. The Lord tells him He will give the land to his
descendants.

Moses' relationship with the Lord was one in which the Lord
spoke to him "as a man speaks to his friend" (Exodus 33:11). The
Lord buries His servant in an unknown location in a valley in Moab.
Even as the people had wept thirty days for Aaron, they now weep
thirty days for Moses.

Moses dies with the knowledge that the Lord has chosen Joshua
and Eleazar to provide the strong leadership that would be needed
when the people cross into the Promised Land. Although Moses does
not enter the Promised Land in his lifetime, Bible commentators point
out that Moses is seen again in the Promised Land long afterward by
three of Jesus' disciples—Peter, James, and John. On a mountaintop in

the Promised Land, they see the Lord Jesus transfigured and speaking with Moses and Elijah (Matthew 17:3).

Reflection: How would you like to be able to describe your relationship with the Lord at the end of your life?

THERE REMAINS YET VERY MUCH LAND

Now Joshua was old and advanced in years, and the LORD said to him, "You are old and advanced in years, and there remains yet very much land to possess."

—Joshua 13:1

After the death of Moses, Joshua leads the Israelites across the Jordan River into the Promised Land. Even as the Lord enabled the Israelites to cross on dry ground when He parted the Red Sea, the Lord enables the next generation to cross the Jordan River on dry ground. He holds back the flowing waters until all have crossed over. Joshua sets up twelve stones from the Jordan, representing the twelve tribes of Israel, as a memorial to remind the people and future generations of the Lord's power and faithfulness.

When Israel reaches Jericho, the Lord instructs Joshua to march once a day around the city for six days. Joshua tells the people to march silently those six days. On the seventh day the people are instructed to march seven times around the city and then shout when the priests blow the trumpets. The people do so, and the walls of Jericho fall. Its inhabitants are slain, and the city is burned. Only Rahab and her family are spared, for earlier she had risked her life and saved two men sent to spy for Israel. Then Israel eventually destroys the city of Ai.

The people of Gibeon make peace with the Israelites through deception, so a coalition of Canaanites prepares to assault Gibeon.

Joshua comes to the aid of Gibeon, and the Lord causes hailstones to kill many of the enemy. The Lord then grants Joshua's request that the sun stand still until the enemy is annihilated. The Bible describes the uniqueness of that day as the time "when the LORD heeded the voice of a man" (Joshua 10:14).

God blesses the leadership of Joshua. Conquest follows conquest, yet much remains to be done. The Lord gives the aged Joshua detailed instructions on dividing the conquered land among the tribes. Regarding the inhabitants in the land not yet possessed, the Lord tells Joshua, "I myself will drive them out from before the people of Israel" (Joshua 13:6). The Lord gives the elderly Joshua the knowledge that He will complete the work that remains.

Reflection: Describe a man or woman you have known whom God has used in leadership very late in life.

"And now, behold, the LORD has kept me [Caleb] alive, just as he said, these forty-five years since the time that the LORD spoke this word to Moses, while Israel walked in the wilderness. And now, behold, I am this day eighty-five years old. I am still as strong today as I was in the day that Moses sent me; my strength now is as my strength was then, for war and for going and coming."

—Joshua 14:10–11

Caleb's strength "for war and for going and coming" remains undiminished many years after he and Joshua explored the land and tried unsuccessfully to convince the Israelites to trust God and not to fear the inhabitants in the Promised Land. Caleb now declares he is as strong as he ever was in his younger years. His physical strength at eighty-five illustrates that God can bless faithful warriors in ways they may not anticipate.

Forty-five years earlier, Moses had declared to Caleb, "Surely the land on which your foot has trodden shall be an inheritance for you and your children forever, because you have wholly followed the LORD my God" (Joshua 14:9). Now Joshua grants Caleb the hill country that Caleb requests—land possessed by the fierce Anakim, whose mere name had caused sheer terror among the previous generation of Israelites.

Caleb receives Joshua's blessing along with an inheritance that includes the city of Hebron. Caleb gives his daughter as a wife to Othniel when Othniel captures Debir. Caleb's daughter then approaches her father, asking for springs of water in addition to the land given to her husband. Caleb grants the request, and so Caleb administers the inheritance Moses had promised that the Lord would give to Caleb and his children.

Reflection: Have you known seniors to whom God has given exceptional physical strength to serve him?

THE WAY OF ALL THE EARTH

Day 25

And now I am about to go the way of all the earth, and you know in your hearts and souls, all of you, that not one word has failed of all the good things that the LORD your God promised concerning you. All have come to pass for you; not one of them has failed.

—Joshua 23:14

Knowing he is going to die soon, Joshua addresses the people whom he has led so faithfully. His last words focus on the reliability of the words the Lord has spoken to His people. Joshua reminds them that the Lord has protected and delivered them on numerous occasions. The Lord's goodness is obvious as they survey their new homes. Through Joshua, the Lord tells them: "I gave you a land on which you had not labored and cities that you had not built, and you dwell in them. You eat the fruit of the vineyards and olive orchards that you did not plant" (Joshua 24:13).

The people are warned not to serve false gods. Joshua challenges the Israelites to choose whom they will serve and declares, "But as for me and my house, we will serve the LORD" (Joshua 24:15). The people respond emphatically that they too will serve the Lord. Joshua makes a covenant with them. He records the words in the Book of the Law of God and sets a large stone near the sanctuary to remind the people of God's words spoken to them.

The people then leave and go to the portions of land they have inherited from the Lord. Joshua dies at the age of 110 and is buried in the land he has inherited. The book of Joshua concludes by noting the inheritances of two former leaders: Joseph and Eleazar. The bones of Joseph are buried in the land bought by Jacob and inherited by Joseph's descendants, and the body of Eleazar, the high priest, is buried in the land given to his son.

Reflection: What can you do to guard the spiritual inheritance God has given you?

CALL ME MARA

Day 26

She said to them, "Do not call me Naomi; call me Mara, for the Almighty has dealt very bitterly with me. I went away full, and the LORD has brought me back empty. Why call me Naomi, when the LORD has testified against me and the Almighty has brought calamity upon me?"

—Ruth 1:20–21

Naomi has so many good expectations. She expects the blessing of children with her husband. They do have two sons, and the family journeys to Moab when famine strikes Bethlehem. Her husband dies, and her sons marry Moabite women, Orpah and Ruth. Naomi then expects the blessing of grandchildren, but within ten years both sons die childless.

Naomi feels a sense of overwhelming loss for herself and her daughters-in-law. She urges them not to return with her to Bethlehem but to remain in Moab and find husbands. She emphasizes that she is "too old to have a husband," for she can no longer bear children (Ruth 1:12). Naomi states that the Lord is afflicting her. She mourns over the collapse of her family.

Her daughter-in-law Ruth, nevertheless, returns to Bethlehem with Naomi. Ruth eventually marries Boaz, a man of integrity, and they have a son, Obed. The women around Naomi declare that the Lord has blessed her. They tell her that her grandson will be "a restorer of life and a nourisher of your old age" (Ruth 4:15).

Neither Naomi nor the women around her can foresee that Obed will become the father of Jesse, who will become the father of David. The gospel of Matthew traces the genealogy of Jesus Christ to Obed. Naomi, the woman who once called herself "bitter," has been blessed by the Lord far more than she knows.

Reflection: Do you remember a time or times when the Lord used others to comfort you?

HE KEPT HEARING ALL THAT HIS SONS WERE DOING

Day 27

> *Now Eli was very old, and he kept hearing all that his sons were doing to all Israel, and how they lay with the women who were serving at the entrance to the tent of meeting. And he said to them, "Why do you do such things? For I hear of your evil doings from all these people. No, my sons; it is no good report that I hear the people of the LORD spreading abroad. If someone sins against a man, God will mediate for him, but if someone sins against the LORD, who can intercede for him?" But they would not listen to the voice of their father, for it was the will of the LORD to put them to death.*

> —I Samuel 2:22–25

Eli took no corrective action. God sends a man of God to Eli with thought-provoking words: "Why then do you scorn my sacrifices and my offerings . . . and honor your sons above me by fattening yourselves on the choicest parts of every offering of my people Israel?" (I Samuel 2:29). The Lord warns that judgment is coming upon his family.

At this time the boy Samuel is serving the Lord under Eli's supervision. The Lord alerts Samuel that He is going to judge Eli's house. When Samuel tells Eli what the Lord has said, Eli responds, "It is the LORD. Let him do what seems good to him" (I Samuel 3:18). Samuel grows into a godly man recognized as a prophet of the Lord.

War erupts between Israel and the Philistines, which results in the death of thousands of Israelites. The Philistines seize the ark of God, and Eli's two sons die. A messenger brings the catastrophic news to Eli, who is blind. Upon hearing that the ark of God has been seized by the Philistines, the ninety-eight-year-old Eli falls backward and breaks his neck. He has judged Israel for forty years. Tragically, his life ends with the news of personal and national calamity.

Reflection: Remembering Jesus' teaching about the prodigal son in Luke 15:11-32, how might someone pray for a prodigal son or daughter?

YET HIS SONS DID NOT WALK IN HIS WAYS

Day 28

> *When Samuel became old, he made his sons judges over Israel. The name of his firstborn son was Joel, and the name of his second, Abijah; they were judges in Beersheba. Yet his sons did not walk in his ways but turned aside after gain. They took bribes and perverted justice.*

—I Samuel 8:1–3

The elders of Israel approach Samuel, expressing concern that Samuel's sons will continue to lead Israel astray when Samuel dies. They ask, "Now appoint for us a king to judge us like all the nations" (I Samuel 8:5).

Unlike Eli, who dishonored the Lord, Samuel remains faithful. The people do not want Samuel's sons to judge them, but also they definitely desire to be "like all the nations." Their request troubles Samuel, but the Lord tells him, "[T]hey have not rejected you, but they have rejected me from being king over them" (I Samuel 8:7). Samuel is included in a list of faithful men and women in the eleventh chapter of the book of Hebrews.

Even after Samuel conveys the Lord's warning about the absolute power that a human king will exercise over them, the people insist on having a king. So the Lord tells Samuel to anoint Saul as king, and Saul wages war against Israel's enemies. Because the Amalekites had ambushed the people of Israel when they left Egypt, the Lord commands Saul to destroy all the Amalekites and all their livestock. However, Saul and the people spare the Amalekite king and spare sheep and oxen to sacrifice to the Lord.

Samuel announces to Saul, "Because you have rejected the word of the LORD, he has also rejected you from being king" (1 Samuel 15:23). The Lord then tells Samuel to anoint David privately. The shepherd boy, who had watched over his father's sheep, experiences success in all that he does. Finally Saul's escalating jealousy forces David to flee and seek refuge in the wilderness with a band of men. Samuel dies during this time.

Whatever disappointment Samuel feels regarding his own sons and Saul, Samuel remains faithful to the Lord. Upon his death all the Israelites gather and mourn the loss of this faithful servant.

Reflection: What might encourage an older man or woman to persevere and serve the Lord wholeheartedly despite discouraging circumstances?

COME OVER WITH ME

Now Barzillai the Gileadite had come down from Rogelim, and he went on with the king to the Jordan, to escort him over the Jordan. Barzillai was a very aged man, eighty years old. He had provided the king [King David] with food while he stayed at Mahanaim, for he was a very wealthy man. And the king said to Barzillai, "Come over with me, and I will provide for you with me in Jerusalem."

—2 Samuel 19:31–33

At the age of eighty, Barzillai is offered the opportunity to travel with King David to Jerusalem and enjoy life in the palace there. During the revolt against David by his son Absalom, Barzillai had provided food to David and his men in the wilderness. Now David expresses his appreciation as he and Barzillai prepare to cross the Jordan River.

Barzillai, a man of wealth, shares with the king that at eighty he can no longer appreciate fine food or drink. It is hard for him to hear the songs of singers. Barzillai asks the king to allow him to return to his own home. He wants to die in his city where his mother and father are buried.

Barzillai offers to go a little distance across the Jordan with the king and then return to his own home. He asks if his servant Chimham, whom some believe to be Barzillai's son, may go with David to Jerusalem in Barzillai's place. David responds that he will do whatever Barzillai asks. After the king crosses the Jordan, he blesses Barzillai, who then returns to the familiar place he calls home.

Barzillai displays much wisdom. He has supported David, the Lord's anointed, by assisting David in the wilderness. Recognizing his own limitations at his age, Barzillai now declines the king's offer of life in a palace. Yet he diplomatically asks if the king will accept his servant Chimham in his place. Thus Barzillai enables the king to repay a debt, and Chimham gains a position of favor with the king.

David never forgets the way Barzillai supported him in his time of need. When David is dying, he gives instructions regarding Barzillai's family to his son Solomon, "But deal loyally with the sons of Barzillai the Gileadite, and let them be among those who eat at your table, for with such loyalty they met me when I fled from Absalom your brother" (I Kings 2:7).

Reflection: If an elderly person is able to continue to live in a familiar environment, what might be some advantages in doing so?

MY OWN EYES SEEING IT

Day 30

And the king [David] bowed himself on the bed. And the king also said, "Blessed be the LORD, the God of Israel, who has granted someone to sit on my throne this day, my own eyes seeing it."

—I Kings 1:47–48

Several of David's sons cause him immense sorrow. His daughter Tamar is raped by her half-brother Amnon. Later David's son Absalom avenges his sister Tamar by murdering Amnon. Eventually Absalom seizes power. To avoid widespread bloodshed in Jerusalem, David hastily flees the city until Absalom is defeated and killed.

When David is old, his oldest living son, Adonijah, attempts to seize the throne despite Solomon being recognized as David's chosen heir. Solomon's mother, Bathsheba, and the prophet Nathan hear about Adonijah's plot and alert David. David has the priest Zadok and the prophet Nathan anoint Solomon in a public ceremony, and Solomon takes his place on the throne as the newly anointed king.

Having ruled Israel for forty years, David has seen much turmoil in his family and kingdom. Now at seventy years of age, he blesses the Lord for allowing him to see his son Solomon anointed as king and sitting on the throne. David begins his final instructions to Solomon by saying, "I am about to go the way of all the earth" (I Kings 2:2).

Earlier in David's life, he wrote a psalm asking for deliverance from the wicked and from those who are entirely satisfied with what the world offers. David concludes the psalm by declaring what will satisfy him ultimately: "As for me, I shall behold your face in righteousness; when I awake, I shall be satisfied with your likeness" (Psalm 17:15).

Reflection: If you were to have the opportunity to share with others what will truly satisfy you, what would you say?

BECAUSE THIS WAS IN YOUR HEART

Day 31

> *God answered Solomon: "Because this was in your heart, and you have not asked for possessions, wealth, honor, or the life of those who hate you, and have not even asked for long life, but have asked for wisdom and knowledge for yourself that you may govern my people over whom I have made you king, wisdom and knowledge are granted to you."*

—2 Chronicles 1:11–12

Solomon's request for wisdom and knowledge pleases God. Unfortunately, although given wisdom and knowledge to govern God's people, Solomon chooses to marry women from nations where idols are worshiped. Eventually he accumulates 700 wives and 300 concubines, and he builds altars for them to worship their false gods. The Bible records the impact of Solomon's marriages to idol worshipers: "For when Solomon was old his wives turned away his heart after other gods, and his heart was not wholly true to the LORD his God, as was the heart of David his father" (1 Kings 11:4).

Solomon experiences turmoil in his later years, yet God tells him: "I will not tear away all the kingdom, but I will give one tribe to your son, for the sake of David my servant and for the sake of Jerusalem that I have chosen" (1 Kings 11:13).

The book of Ecclesiastes, written probably by Solomon in his later years, ends with a poem that can be viewed as an allegory about aging. The house mentioned in the poem may represent the human body. Its windows may symbolize a person's dimming eyesight, and the trembling "keepers of the house" perhaps represent trembling hands and arms. The poem describes details such as getting up when the birds sing and being afraid of heights.

Solomon offers advice to the young at the end of Ecclesiastes: "Remember also your Creator in the days of your youth, before the evil days come and the years draw near of which you will say, 'I have no pleasure in them'" (Ecclesiastes 12:1). Solomon recognizes a distinction between a person's body and spirit: "[A]nd the dust returns to the earth as it was, and the spirit returns to God who gave it" (Ecclesiastes 12:7).

Strife characterizes the final years of Solomon's forty-year reign. After he dies, the kingdom splits. The tribes in the north follow Jeroboam as king. The southern tribes of Judah and Benjamin follow Solomon's son Rehoboam.

Reflection: In addition to romantic attachments, what might cause a person to follow after other gods in his or her later years?

SET YOUR HOUSE IN ORDER *Day 32*

In those days Hezekiah became sick and was at the point of death.
And Isaiah the prophet the son of Amoz came to him and said
to him, "Thus says the LORD, 'Set your house in order, for you
shall die; you shall not recover.'" Then Hezekiah turned his face
to the wall and prayed to the LORD, saying, "Now, O LORD,
please remember how I have walked before you in faithfulness and
with a whole heart, and have done what is good in your sight."
And Hezekiah wept bitterly.

—2 Kings 20:1–3

Hezekiah was the son of King Ahaz, who "burned his sons as an offering, according to the abominations of the nations whom the LORD drove out before the people of Israel" (2 Chronicles 28:3). However, Hezekiah "did what was right in the eyes of the LORD" (2 Kings 18:3). Upon hearing from Isaiah that Hezekiah's own death is imminent, he weeps and prays.

As Isaiah is leaving the palace, the Lord instructs him to return and tell Hezekiah that his prayer has been heard and Hezekiah will be healed. The Lord informs Hezekiah that he will live fifteen more years and that the Lord will deliver Hezekiah and Jerusalem from the Assyrians for the sake of David.

The Bible states that Hezekiah, who has immense wealth, later becomes prideful and displays his wealth to dignitaries visiting from Babylon. Isaiah confronts Hezekiah regarding his foolish pride and prophesies that the Babylonians in the future will capture Jerusalem. Hezekiah feels thankful that despite his foolishness "there will be peace and security in my days" (2 Kings 20:19).

After the death of Hezekiah, his son Manasseh and grandson Amon do evil in the Lord's sight. Nevertheless, Hezekiah's great-grandson, Josiah, becomes king and does what is pleasing to God.

Reflection: If you knew God was granting you fifteen more years to live, what would you do with those years?

OLD MEN WHO HAD SEEN THE FIRST HOUSE

But many of the priests and Levites and heads of fathers' houses, old men who had seen the first house, wept with a loud voice when they saw the foundation of this house being laid, though many shouted aloud for joy, so that the people could not distinguish the sound of the joyful shout from the sound of the people's weeping, for the people shouted with a great shout, and the sound was heard far away.

—Ezra 3:12–13

Fifty years after the destruction of Solomon's magnificent temple, old men remember its incomparable beauty and grandeur. They remember bringing offerings for the altar located near the bronze sea. They recall gazing upward at the hundreds of sculpted pomegranates which encircled two bronze pillars at the temple entrance. Inside, the walls and the floors had been overlaid with gold. In the Holy Place were objects of gold, such as the altar, tables for the bread of the Presence, lampstands, and bowls.

Moreover, they remember that only the high priest could enter the Most Holy Place once a year on the Day of Atonement. He entered with blood to make atonement for his sins and the sins of the people. Within the Most Holy Place was the ark of God covered on the inside and outside with gold. Above the cover of the ark two golden cherubim with outspread wings faced each other. The ark contained two stone tablets with the Ten Commandments given to Moses on Mt. Sinai by the Lord.

The older generation had worshiped at Solomon's temple, witnessed its destruction by the Babylonians, and suffered as captives in a foreign land and culture. Now, back in their homeland, they weep in remembrance, and they shout for joy in anticipation of rebuilding a place to worship the Lord.

When the second temple is finally completed, the people offer sacrifices and keep the Passover. They keep "the Feast of Unleavened Bread seven days with joy, for the LORD had made them joyful" (Ezra 6:22).

Reflection: Do you know of a situation where an older person has wept for joy upon seeing the Lord accomplish what seemed impossible in his or her lifetime?

FOR I KNOW THAT MY REDEEMER LIVES

For I know that my Redeemer
lives,
and at the last he will stand
upon the earth.
And after my skin has been
thus destroyed,
yet in my flesh I shall see
God,
whom I shall see for myself,
and my eyes shall behold,
and not another.
My heart faints within me!

—Job 19:25–27

In addition to immense wealth, Job has seven sons and three daughters whom he treasures. Defiantly, Satan challenges the Lord, asserting that Job will curse the Lord if Job loses what he has. The Lord grants Satan power over what Job has, and Satan takes the lives of Job's livestock, servants, and ten children. When Job does not curse God, Satan asks for and receives permission from the Lord to strike Job's body, but not to take Job's life. Although stricken with painful sores all over his body, Job does not speak against God.

Job's friends suggest reasons for his suffering, but their reasoning is flawed. They do not realize God is permitting His servant to be tested. Ultimately the Lord Himself speaks to Job, and Job humbly acknowledges God's greatness: "I had heard of you by the hearing of the ear, but now my eye sees you; therefore I despise myself, and repent in dust and ashes" (Job 42:5–6). The Bible does not say Job is ever told the reason for his suffering.

The Lord blesses Job's later years even more than his earlier years. Job dies at an old age, blessed to see four generations of his family. Job's earlier declaration becomes reality: "[W]hen he has tried me, I shall come out as gold" (Job 23:10).

Reflection: Have you known someone who endured horrendous suffering and came out as gold later in life?

THE DAYS THAT WERE FORMED FOR ME

Your eyes saw my unformed
  substance;
in your book were written,
  every one of them,
the days that were formed
  for me,
when as yet there was none
  of them.

—Psalm 139:16

In his psalms, David reflects on life and death. He declares God sees even our "unformed substance." David would like to know how many days he will live, but he acknowledges the Lord's sovereignty: "My times are in your hand" (Psalm 31:15). Times of uncertainty, disappointment, and danger prepare David to trust the Lord in his early and later years. He learns to look to Him for peace as well as protection: "In peace I will both lie down and sleep; for you alone, O LORD, make me dwell in safety" (Psalm 4:8).

Although David, a man of war, desires to build a house for the Lord, the Lord tells him He has chosen Solomon, a man of peace, to build His temple and rule His people after David's reign. To assist his son Solomon, King David gathers materials for the massive building project: gold, silver, bronze, iron, wood, onyx, precious stones, and marble slabs.

David understands he is destined eventually to live in another house:

> Surely goodness and mercy
>> shall follow me
> all the days of my life,
> and I shall dwell in the house
>> of the LORD
> forever.

(Psalm 23:6)

Bible translators state that the Hebrew word "follow" can be translated as "pursue." In other words, when the Lord is our Shepherd, His goodness and mercy pursue us all the days of our lives.

Reflection: What memories come to mind about God's goodness pursuing you all the days of your life?

UNTIL I PROCLAIM YOUR MIGHT *Day 36*

O God, from my youth you
have taught me,
and I still proclaim your
wondrous deeds.
So even to old age and gray
hairs,
O God, do not forsake me,
until I proclaim your might
to another generation,
your power to all those to
come.

—Psalm 71:17–18

The unnamed psalmist in Psalm 71 views himself as having a responsibility to declare the might and power of the Lord to the next generation. Reflecting on God's faithfulness, the psalmist shares that he has trusted the Lord from his youth. He asks the Lord to continue to be his strength in old age when his human strength may fail. He trusts God to revive him again and promises to sing to God, who has redeemed his soul.

Psalm 92, also written by an unnamed psalmist, refers to fruitfulness in old age. The psalmist compares the righteous to trees "planted in the house of the LORD":

They still bear fruit in old age;
    they are ever full of sap and
        green,
to declare that the LORD is
        upright;
    he is my rock, and there is
        no unrighteousness in
        him.

(Psalm 92:14–15)

Both Psalm 71 and 92 present old age as a time when a person can praise God for who He is and what He has done.

Reflection: What are some of your favorite songs of praise about who God is and what He has done?

THE WISE WILL INHERIT HONOR

Toward the scorners he is
    scornful,
   but to the humble he gives
    favor.
The wise will inherit honor,
   but fools get disgrace.

—Proverbs 3:34–35

The word "inherit" is commonly associated with tangible possessions—property, personal belongings, or money—received from a person upon his or her death. The Bible describes both tangible and intangible inheritances.

In the book of Proverbs, written primarily by Solomon, intangible inheritance is examined. Wisdom is contrasted with foolishness. A person's inheritance of honor or disgrace depends upon whether one chooses wisdom or foolishness. The writer states that "the wise will inherit honor" and counsels young men to listen to the older people in their lives to gain wisdom.

In the beginning of Proverbs, the writer personifies wisdom as a woman. The book concludes with a description of the wife who "opens her mouth with wisdom" (Proverbs 31:26). Acknowledging that beauty fades with time, the writer emphasizes that a woman who fears the Lord deserves praise: "Charm is deceitful, and beauty is vain, but a woman who fears the LORD is to be praised" (Proverbs 31:30). A woman who honors the Lord inherits honor.

The tangible inheritance of land is a recurring topic throughout the Bible. The people of Israel inherit the Promised Land from God, and detailed inheritance laws maintain the inherited land of each tribe and family. Moses tells the people of Israel that they are God's inheritance: "But the LORD has taken you and brought you out of the iron furnace, out of Egypt, to be a people of his own inheritance, as you are this day" (Deuteronomy 4:20).

Many generations later, David shares his joy that the Lord is his inheritance:

> The LORD is my chosen por-
> tion and my cup;
> you hold my lot.
> The lines have fallen for me
> in pleasant places;
> indeed, I have a beautiful
> inheritance.

> (Psalm 16:5–6)

Reflection: Describe elderly men and women you have known who have inherited honor.

EVERYTHING BEAUTIFUL IN ITS TIME

He has made everything beautiful in its time. Also, he has put eternity into man's heart, yet so that he cannot find out what God has done from the beginning to the end.

—Ecclesiastes 3:11

The author of Ecclesiastes, who calls himself the Preacher, begins by proclaiming "All is vanity" (Ecclesiastes 1:2). Bible commentators offer various perspectives on the statement. Some believe the statement should be translated as "All is utterly meaningless." Others interpret the statement as "All is utterly meaningless without God." Because the word "vanity" indicates "breath" or "vapor," some commentators suggest "All is quickly passing." They believe the writer is urging people to appreciate their lives since their lives are quickly passing.

Quite likely "the Preacher" is Solomon, in his later years, addressing issues with which an elderly person may struggle. For instance, to whom should a person leave his or her home, belongings, or money upon death? The observation is made that a person may work hard to accumulate possessions but must leave everything to others when he or she dies. Nevertheless, Solomon views doing good and enjoying the fruits of one's labor as a blessing from God.

Solomon recognizes a rhythm in life: "For everything there is a season, and a time for every matter under heaven: a time to be born, and a time to die" (Ecclesiastes 3:1–2). Throughout his discourse, he

84

presents the benefits of wisdom with unique observations, such as his assertion about the day when a person with a good name dies: "A good name is better than precious ointment, and the day of death than the day of birth" (Ecclesiastes 7:1). In other words, when a person with a good name dies, on that day he or she leaves for others a legacy "better than precious ointment."

Reflection: What kind of legacy "better than precious ointment" would you like to leave?

I WILL CARRY AND WILL SAVE *Day 39*

Listen to me, O house of Jacob,
    all the remnant of the house
        of Israel,
who have been borne by me
        from before your birth,
    carried from the womb;
even to your old age, I am he,
    and to gray hairs I will carry
        you.
I have made, and I will bear;
    I will carry and will save.

—Isaiah 46:3–4

The act of "carrying" appears in various places in the Bible. Moses reminds the Israelites that God carried His children in the wilderness. David asks God to shepherd His people and carry them forever. Jesus presents a parable about a shepherd who finds his lost sheep, lifts it joyfully onto his shoulders, and carries it home.

In Isaiah, God describes Himself carrying His people from the womb to old age. He portrays an intimate, protective relationship. Isaiah points out that the Lord carries for them that which they cannot carry: "Surely he has borne our griefs and carried our sorrows ... and the Lord has laid on him the iniquity of us all" (Isaiah 53:4–6). Isaiah's prophetic words foretell that on the cross Jesus would bear our sin—"the iniquity of us all." His blood would cover our sin and make it possible for us to ask and receive God's forgiveness.

God promises His people in Isaiah that He will continue to carry them and care for them as they grow old: "[T]o gray hairs I will carry you. I have made, and I will bear; I will carry and will save."

Reflection: Can you recall the comfort you felt as a child when a family member or other person carried you?

THE YOUNG MEN AND THE OLD   *Day 40*

Then shall the young women
rejoice in the dance,
and the young men and the
old shall be merry.
I will turn their mourning
into joy;
I will comfort them, and
give them gladness for
sorrow.

—Jeremiah 31:13

Jeremiah prophesies for many years that judgment is coming upon Judah because the people have turned away from God and are worshiping idols. He points out the utter foolishness of worshiping idols—objects of wood or stone that have been made by human hands. The contrast could not be more obvious: God carries His sons and daughters, but those who worship idols have to carry the idols they worship.

When Nebuchadnezzar's army breaks through Jerusalem's walls in 586 B.C., his army loots and burns the temple. Many of Judah's leaders had been taken earlier to Babylon, and now others are taken into captivity too. Jeremiah grieves over the young and the old slain by the sword in the streets of Jerusalem.

Jeremiah realizes that after captivity and exile the Lord will bring His people back to their homeland. He will "comfort them, and give them gladness for sorrow." In the midst of suffering and sorrow, Jeremiah affirms God's love, mercy, and faithfulness:

> The steadfast love of the
> LORD never ceases;
> his mercies never come to
> an end;
> they are new every morning;
> great is your faithfulness.

(Lamentations 3:22–23)

The faithful prophet dies in exile in Egypt at an old age.

Reflection: Do you have a childhood memory of grieving with an elderly person?

I AM AN OLD MAN

Day 41

> *And Zechariah said to the angel, "How shall I know this? For I am an old man, and my wife is advanced in years."*

—Luke 1:18

Zechariah, a priest, is burning incense in the temple when an angel appears. The angel informs him that he and his wife Elizabeth will have a son, whom they are to name John: "[H]e will be filled with the Holy Spirit, even from his mother's womb. And he will turn many of the children of Israel to the Lord their God, and he will go before him in the spirit and power of Elijah ..." (Luke 1:15–17).

Zechariah responds by questioning how this can be possible since he and his wife are old. In the temple of God, in the presence of an angel, a priest is doubting an angel's message. The angel identifies himself as Gabriel and says he has been sent to bring the good news to Zechariah. However, because Zechariah has not believed the message, Gabriel states that Zechariah will be unable to speak "until the day that these things take place" (Luke 1:20). When his son is born, Zechariah's voice returns and he blesses the Lord:

> Blessed is the Lord God of
>   Israel,
>   for he has visited and
>   redeemed his people
> and has raised up a horn of

salvation for us
in the house of his servant
David.

(Luke 1:68–69)

For the rest of his life, Zechariah lives with the knowledge that God has visited His people and blessed "an old man" and a woman "advanced in years" with a son who "will be called the prophet of the Most High" (Luke 1:76).

Reflection: When have you experienced that God's timing can be very different from your timing?

FILLED WITH THE HOLY SPIRIT — *Day 42*

And when Elizabeth heard the greeting of Mary, the baby leaped in her womb. And Elizabeth was filled with the Holy Spirit.

—Luke 1:41

The Bible describes Elizabeth and her husband, Zechariah, as "righteous before God, walking blamelessly in all the commandments and statutes of the Lord" (Luke 1:6). When the angel Gabriel tells Zechariah that he and Elizabeth will have a son whom they are to call John, Gabriel says, "[Y]our prayer has been heard" (Luke 1:13).

After Mary conceives the long-awaited Messiah, she travels to the home of Elizabeth, her cousin, who has become pregnant. As Mary enters Elizabeth's home and greets her, Elizabeth exclaims that she feels her baby leap for joy. Filled with the Holy Spirit, Elizabeth blesses Mary: "Blessed are you among women, and blessed is the fruit of your womb! And why is this granted to me that the mother of my Lord should come to me?" (Luke 1:42–43). Mary responds with joy: "My soul magnifies the Lord, and my spirit rejoices in God my Savior" (Luke 1:46–47).

Mary stays with Elizabeth about three months before going back home. After Elizabeth gives birth to a son, family and friends celebrate the birth and gather for his circumcision. They want to give him his father's name, but Elizabeth says he is to have the name John. They object to her choice of names and ask Zechariah, who has not been able to speak since the day he doubted Gabriel's message. When

Zechariah confirms the name by writing on a tablet, instantly his voice returns. Their neighbors become fearful, and those who hear about the incident wonder, "What then will this child be?" (Luke 1:65–66).

Regarding John's early years, the Bible states that "the child grew and became strong in spirit, and he was in the wilderness until the day of his public appearance to Israel" (Luke 1:80).

Reflection: Do you know someone in ministry who credits parents or grandparents "advanced in years" for preparing him or her to serve the Lord?

FASTING AND PRAYER

And there was a prophetess, Anna, the daughter of Phanuel, of the tribe of Asher. She was advanced in years, having lived with her husband seven years from when she was a virgin, and then as a widow until she was eighty-four. She did not depart from the temple, worshiping with fasting and prayer night and day.

—Luke 2:36–37

Anna's life revolves around fasting and prayer in the temple. The temple's outer court, the Court of the Gentiles, is open to everyone. The temple's inner courts are accessible only to those who are Jewish. Its Women's Court is accessible to women and men, and the Court of Israel is restricted to men. The Court of the Priests, with the altar for burnt offering and the laver for washing, is located in front of the sanctuary and around its sides.

Scripture tells us that the Holy Spirit guides a man named Simeon into the temple, where he encounters Joseph, Mary, and the baby Jesus. Joseph and Mary are bringing their firstborn son to present Him to the Lord and to offer a sacrifice of a pair of turtledoves or two young pigeons.

The Holy Spirit has made known to Simeon that "he would not see death before he had seen the Lord's Christ" (Luke 2:26). Seeing the baby, Simeon takes Him in his arms. He blesses God and identifies the baby as God's salvation: "a light for revelation to the Gentiles, and for glory to your people Israel" (Luke 2:32).

Anna, too, speaks about the Lord in the temple courtyard: "And coming up at that very hour she began to give thanks to God and to speak of him to all who were waiting for the redemption of Jerusalem" (Luke 2:38). God gives this very old and faithful servant the special honor of speaking about Him in the temple where she has fasted and prayed.

Reflection: Describe a time when you recognized that the Lord was showing you an answer to your prayers.

"Truly, truly, I say to you [Peter], when you were young, you used to dress yourself and walk wherever you wanted, but when you are old, you will stretch out your hands, and another will dress you and carry you where you do not want to go."(This he said to show by what kind of death he was to glorify God.) And after saying this, he said to him, "Follow me."

—John 2I:18–I9

After the Resurrection, Jesus speaks to Peter about the death Peter will experience when he is old—the death by which he will "glorify God." Jesus concludes with two words for Peter regarding the path that lies ahead: "Follow me."

Toward the end of his life, Peter refers to this conversation with the Lord Jesus in a letter written to believers: "I think it right, as long as I am in this body, to stir you up by way of reminder, since I know that the putting off of my body will be soon, as our Lord Jesus Christ made clear to me" (2 Peter I:13–I4).

Knowing he will die for his faith in his Savior and Lord, Peter can still rejoice in the midst of his trials. He remembers the miracles the crowds saw and the teachings the crowds heard. However, Peter also remembers the personal moments away from the crowds when Jesus was teaching and preparing his disciples to share the good news of God's grace. He describes hearing God's voice from heaven when Jesus was transfigured on a mountaintop. Peter knows he will die for his faith in his Savior and Lord, yet Peter also knows with certainty that he has "an inheritance that is imperishable, undefiled, and unfading, kept in heaven" (I Peter 1:4).

Reflection: How might it bless a person to know he or she will be leaving the earth soon to dwell in heaven?

THE GOSPEL OF THE GRACE OF GOD

And now, behold, I am going to Jerusalem, constrained by the Spirit, not knowing what will happen to me there, except that the Holy Spirit testifies to me in every city that imprisonment and afflictions await me. But I do not account my life of any value nor as precious to myself, if only I may finish my course and the ministry that I received from the Lord Jesus, to testify to the gospel of the grace of God.

—Acts 20:22–24

Before Saul encounters the Lord Jesus and becomes known as Paul, he was characterized as "still breathing threats and murder against the disciples of the Lord" (Acts 9:1). He asked for and received letters from the high priest to arrest believers in Damascus.

The book of Acts describes Saul's transformation on the road to Damascus:

> . . . suddenly a light from heaven shone around him. And falling to the ground he heard a voice saying to him, "Saul, Saul, why are you persecuting me?" And he said, "Who are you, Lord?" And he said, "I am Jesus, whom you are persecuting." (Acts 9:3-5)

The Lord Jesus instructs Saul to go to the city and await further instructions. Now unable to see, Saul is guided to Damascus where Ananias, a disciple, comes to Saul and lays hands on him. Saul receives his sight again and is baptized. Grace has been given and received.

In Paul's letters to early churches and to Timothy, he compares life to a race, yet not a race for the applause of a crowd or an earthly reward. He shares that he disciplines himself so he may receive the heavenly reward that will come when he completes his race on the earth.

Paul yearns for and anticipates victory even as he suffers for his faith. In 2 Corinthians he writes that he has been persecuted, whipped, imprisoned, beaten with rods, stoned, and shipwrecked. He has known hunger, sleeplessness, weariness, thirst, cold, and exposure. Nevertheless, he writes to the church at Philippi, "But one thing I do: forgetting what lies behind and straining forward to what lies ahead, I press on toward the goal for the prize of the upward call of God in Christ Jesus" (Philippians 3:13–14).

Paul chooses to focus on Jesus and the joy that awaits him upon completion of his race.

Reflection: Looking back at a time of sorrow or suffering in your life, what strengthened you so you could "press on"?

HEIRS OF GOD AND FELLOW HEIRS WITH CHRIST

The Spirit himself bears witness with our spirit that we are children of God, and if children, then heirs—heirs of God and fellow heirs with Christ, provided we suffer with him in order that we may also be glorified with him.

For I consider that the sufferings of this present time are not worth comparing with the glory that is to be revealed to us.

—Romans 8:16–18

We are "heirs of God and fellow heirs with Christ," and our Heavenly Father has told us we have an extraordinary inheritance. We do not need a lawyer to explain the details. God's Word informs us that the inheritance which we begin to receive on the earth will not diminish and will be ours forever.

The apostle Paul writes that "we are more than conquerors through him who loved us" and concludes that nothing "will be able to separate us from the love of God in Christ Jesus our Lord" (Romans 8:37–39). He alludes to his inheritance in a letter to the Philippians: "For me to live is Christ, and to die is gain" (Philippians 1:21).

Paul, a tentmaker, views the body as a tent: "For while we are still in this tent, we groan, being burdened—not that we would be unclothed, but that we would be further clothed, so that what is mortal may be swallowed up by life" (2 Corinthians 5:4). We gain a glorious inheritance when we leave our tents.

Paul emphasizes that we have a spiritual inheritance from God because we are sons and no longer slaves to sin. As children of God, we inherit from our Heavenly Father. We can know with certainty that God is our Father and that we are His heirs: "And because you are sons, God has sent the Spirit of his Son into our hearts, crying, 'Abba! Father!' So you are no longer a slave, but a son, and if a son, then an heir through God" (Galatians 4:6–7).

Reflection: As you reflect on being an heir of God and a fellow heir with Christ, what thoughts come to mind?

WE SHALL ALL BE CHANGED *Day 47*

> *I tell you this, brothers: flesh and blood cannot inherit the kingdom of God, nor does the perishable inherit the imperishable. Behold! I tell you a mystery. We shall not all sleep, but we shall all be changed, in a moment, in the twinkling of an eye, at the last trumpet. For the trumpet will sound, and the dead will be raised imperishable, and we shall be changed.*

—I Corinthians 15:50–52

Paul looks forward to wondrous change even as he struggles with personal challenges, such as a physical problem he calls "a thorn in the flesh": "[A] thorn was given me in the flesh, a messenger of Satan to harass me, to keep me from becoming conceited" (2 Corinthians 12:7). Some believe the thorn may have been a problem with his eyes.

Despite Paul's pleading with the Lord to remove the problem, the thorn remains. The Lord says to him, "My grace is sufficient for you, for my power is made perfect in weakness" (2 Corinthians 12:9). Paul understands and wants the church to understand that suffering can provide opportunities to display the power of Christ.

The Lord prepares Paul for what lies ahead at the end of his life. Paul tells the elders at Ephesus that the Holy Spirit has let him know he will suffer and they will never see him again. Paul accepts the suffering that lies ahead, knowing that immortality and victory also lie ahead: "When the perishable puts on the imperishable, and the mortal puts on immortality, then shall come to pass the saying that is written: 'Death is swallowed up in victory'" (I Corinthians 15:54).

Reflection: Can you recall a time in your life when you recognized God's grace is sufficient?

I HAVE FINISHED THE RACE

Day 48

I have fought the good fight, I have finished the race, I have kept the faith. Henceforth there is laid up for me the crown of righteousness, which the Lord, the righteous judge, will award to me on that Day, and not only to me but also to all who have loved his appearing.

—2 Timothy 4:7–8

Paul and the young Timothy serve together, traveling to places such as Philippi, Thessalonica, Athens, Corinth, Ephesus, and Macedonia. Paul calls Timothy "a true son in the faith" (I Timothy 1:2) and describes Timothy's mother and grandmother as women of faith. Timothy is a young man who can be trusted, and Timothy's friendship definitely encourages the older Paul.

Paul and Timothy live in a culture that associates wisdom with the elderly. In a letter Paul instructs Timothy how to treat younger and older members in the church: "Do not rebuke an older man but encourage him as you would a father, younger men as brothers, older women as mothers, younger women as sisters, in all purity" (I Timothy 5:I–2).

The introductory greeting in Paul's letters to the churches of Philippi and Colossae reveal that Paul and Timothy are in contact during Paul's first imprisonment in Rome. Many Bible scholars believe Paul's second letter to Timothy was written during a later imprisonment in Rome shortly before Paul was martyred. In the letter, Paul urges Timothy, "Do your best to come before winter" (2 Timothy 4:21). The Bible does not mention if Timothy is able to do so.

Paul closes the final letter to Timothy with words of blessing: "The Lord be with your spirit. Grace be with you" (2 Timothy 4:22). Paul, a recipient of God's undeserved love, yearns for others to know the grace of God flowing through their lives.

Reflection: Have you been mentored in ministry by an older person, or have you perhaps mentored a younger person?

WE SHALL BE LIKE HIM

Beloved, we are God's children now, and what we will be has not yet appeared; but we know that when he appears we shall be like him, because we shall see him as he is. And everyone who thus hopes in him purifies himself as he is pure.

—I John 3:2–3

When John writes to believers that "we shall be like Him," he writes as a man who has seen Jesus transfigured on a mountaintop. He has seen Jesus' face shining "like the sun" and His clothes becoming "white as light." Along with Peter and James, John has heard a voice say, "This is my beloved Son, with whom I am well pleased; listen to him" (Matthew 17:5).

When Jesus is nailed to the cross and suffers the agonies of crucifixion, John is standing nearby with the mother of Jesus and a few other women. Jesus directs John to care for His mother Mary as if she were John's own mother. The Bible records that "from that hour the disciple [John] took her to his own home" (John 19:27). John becomes her caregiver.

After the Crucifixion and Resurrection, John understands more fully that following Jesus means taking up one's cross and becoming a servant like Him. He no longer has the attitude he had when he and his brother James asked Jesus if they could sit at His right hand and left hand in His glory. John takes up his cross and serves the Lord for many years, providing vital leadership in the early church.

In addition to writing the gospel of John, he writes three letters included in the New Testament and writes the book of Revelation. In the beginning of Revelation, John mentions he is in exile on the island of Patmos "on account of the word of God and the testimony of Jesus" (Revelation 1:9). In his older years, by the grace of God, John continues to be like a tree "still bear[ing] fruit in old age" (Psalm 92:14).

Reflection: In what ways does John's long life encourage you?

These all died in faith, not having received the things promised, but having seen them and greeted them from afar, and having acknowledged that they were strangers and exiles on the earth. For people who speak thus make it clear that they are seeking a homeland.

—Hebrews 11:13–14

Abel, Enoch, Noah, Abraham, Sarah, and other men and women of faith are described in Hebrews as sojourners or pilgrims on earth. They choose to trust God on their earthly journey, and God is pleased with their trust in Him.

The writer of Hebrews portrays Isaac, Jacob, and Joseph as continuing to trust God at the very end of their lives. By faith Isaac and Jacob bless their families, and by faith Joseph speaks about the people of Israel eventually returning to the Promised Land.

Moses, Rahab, Gideon, Barak, Samson, Jephthah, David, Samuel, and the prophets are also named in Hebrews along with unnamed men and women of faith. Some of them experience extraordinary victories, and some endure excruciating circumstances. They know God will keep His promises, and they look forward to their eternal homeland.

Living life can be like running a race. Living a long life may require the insight and endurance of a marathon runner. Jesus, "the founder and perfecter of our faith," enables us to run the race set before us:

Therefore, since we are surrounded by so great a cloud of witnesses, let us also lay aside every weight, and sin which clings so closely, and let us run with endurance the race that is set before us, looking to Jesus, the founder and perfecter of our faith, who for the joy that was set before him endured the cross, despising the shame, and is seated at the right hand of the throne of God. (Hebrews 12:1–2)

Reflection: How is God enabling you to run with endurance the race set before you?

BENEDICTION FOR A RUNNER
(Psalm 34:8)

May His wind refresh as you run the race
that God Himself has marked out for you.
May His light shine forth as you follow Him,
serving as created to do.

May you taste and see that God is so good.
May you renew your strength in His Word.
May you rest in His love, knowing Jesus is Lord.
May you sing forever to Him.

—Marsha MacLeod

Printed in the United States
By Bookmasters